Chuck
The World's
Greatest
Therapy Dog

Tails of Love:
A Journal
of Chuck Stories

BARBARA WILSON

DEDICATION

Thank you to the healthcare professionals that made our job, and the journey so much fun and meaningful.

A special Paws-up for my Aunt Beverly.

You gave me so much support, encouragement and editing help.

I would not have been able to take on this project without Lola's mom, Asha.

Thank you.

Table of Contents

PROLOGUE

Starting Our Journal

Helping With a Goodbye:

The halls were empty except for a few staff members. It was very quiet and many doors in the hall were closed. This was our second day at the Atrium Health Hospital as a volunteer.

After a while a gentleman came looking for me and asked if I would bring Chuck to the room for his mother and family. He said their mother loved dogs and he wanted her to pet him as she passed into the next world. They were all gathered around her bed to say goodbye.

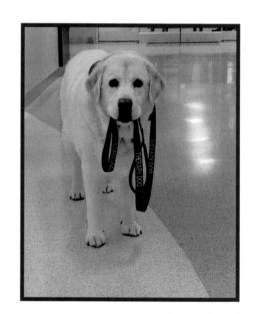

Of course, Chuck did not understand the situation and was happy to attend the gathering. He sweetly stood by her pillow as she stroked his head. They said "Goodbye, Mom".

I emotionally stood at the back of the room.

As I was to experience many times over the years, I observed the power of a therapy dog.

THE WORLD'S GREATEST THERAPY DOG

With no impressive goals or dreams in my life at the time, I decided to create the most special therapy dog... ever.

And I did.

I have a plaque to prove it.

DOGS IN ANCIENT TIMES

They were used in hunting, as guard dogs, and for herding sheep but were also kept as companions. A dog's soul was thought to be constituted of one-third wild beast, one-third human, and **one-third divine** and so dogs were to be treated with proper respect and consideration.

A LITTLE THERAPY DOG HISTORY

Dogs have been providing therapy since the beginning of time, but the first record of a *trained* therapy dog started in 1944 during WWII. A member of MacArthur's 5th Air Force (a photo recon squadron) found a tiny Yorkshire Terrier in a fox hole in New Guinea.

His name was Smoky and he was a calming influence for the soldiers according to an article in

National Geographic.

But first there was Sargeant Stubby....

A Stray Becomes a World War I Military Dog

Sergeant Stubby was a stray bull terrier mix who, in 1917, wandered onto a military training lot in New Haven, Connecticut. There he met Private J. Robert Conroy, a young man in whose company he would travel the world, save lives, and become famous.

Stubby, as the little dog was dubbed, quickly joined the daily routines of Private Conroy's unit, the 26th Yankee Division of the U.S. Army's 102nd Infantry. He entertained the soldiers with antics that included a modified salute with his paw. However, a canine couldn't officially join their ranks. So, when the Yankee Division shipped out one night, Stubby quietly hopped on the train along with them, and then, with Private Conroy's help, stowed away on the troop transport ship.

He soon began to prove his worth on the battlefields. Distinguishing friend from foe by their familiar language and smells, Stubby alerted medics to the cries of wounded soldiers—or stayed with them until they died so they would not be left alone. He led disoriented soldiers back to the trenches. *FamilySearch.com*

CHUCK'S PEDIGREE

Chuck entered our life as a birthday present in 2008. He was a surprise gift for my husband Bob. I brought in this big, bellied puppy, as a special gift. Chuck was born into a bi-racial family, Light Cream Yellow Dad, Deep Black Mom, 6 yellow siblings, 5 coal black siblings. His father was a show champion and his mother looked like she was a mafia boss. His birthplace was around Waynesville, North Carolina – a tar heel to the end. Or is it a tar paw?

ALWAYS A LAB AROUND

I grew up with Labs. As far back as I can remember we had black labs. Ace, Deuce and Trey were the first three. Ace was fierce and protective, Deuce was fun and sweet, Trey wasn't right in the head. Or a Southern saying might be 'His corn bread wasn't cooked in the middle'. As an adult my husband and I had a bold black lab like Ace, his name was Curtiss.

Then our first yellow lab was 'Walt'.

He had a strange trait of ripping hats or visors off people's heads.

He hated head covers.

Friends or family would lean down to say

"hello" and he'd grab their baseball cap.

His claim to fame though was the game **'Flying Puppies"**.

He eventually was able to jump over 7 people.

Walt

THEN CAME THE BIG GUY

Chuck's favorite thing to do through the years was to hang out in the front yard tied to a 10-foot ski rope. While sitting patiently by the sidewalk he waited to say hello. He greeted those that passed by sitting by the sidewalk to say hello, hid in the bushes and jumped out as a good scare tactic, barked at dogs walking by that he didn't like, played with friends … and sometimes he just slept.

That is how he met so many people. Everybody knew Chuck.

We even had lawn parties on his birthday. One of the most anticipated events for neighbors and friends. This is also very good for therapy dog socialization.

DISCOVERY AND THERAPY DOG WORK

This playful, calm personality caught the eye of a neighbor who said that Chuck was a natural for therapy dog work. Like being discovered by a talent agent. The neighbor had owned 4 dogs that went through the process to become a certified Therapy dog. He said he would work with Chuck a little and help me learn how to train him. Thank you, John.

Note that the experts say that the dog needs to have **'it'**. Like a model or actor. The dog can be a loving, sweet pup but they need to be trained. They also need to be over one-year old.

Some people hire a trainer to help them, which is great whether they become certified or not. I found that I could work with Chuck on each task over several months. I will share more on the requirements and how I accomplished training Chuck on my own.

What Is a Therapy Dog?

A therapy dog lends comfort and affection to people in a facility setting or to certain individuals who require visitation to deal with a physical or emotional problem. Therapy dogs are **not service dogs** who provide a specific service for a person with special needs, and who receive full public access per the Americans with Disabilities Act (ADA). They are also not **emotional support animals** who require a prescription from a mental health or health care professional but need no special training or certifications to do their job. *American Kennel Club*

*Sit

*Wait for my command

*Heel

WHY DO DOGS LOVE BEING PET SO MUCH

Petting a dog releases feel-good hormones like oxytocin in both the dog and the person doing the petting, creating a positive bonding experience. Additionally, dogs have scent glands on their heads, so being petted in that area may also be a form of social bonding and communication for them. *Quora.com*

Think of animals at the zoo like monkeys. They are grooming each other as do other animals. With dogs, it is kind of a one-way street – we groom them.

There are also places where you should not pet a dog. They especially do not like the hand of a stranger coming up over their head when approached.

FIRST STEP – THERAPY DOG CERTIFICATION

Falling Asleep During a Test... and Still Passing

On any official therapy dog website there is a list of actions they need to do without fail. Fail one...and you don't pass.

A tough one that I thought we would fail is that the dog should ignore food. Not possible, I thought. You walk over a bowl full of food and keep going. I hesitated over the bowl the first time and Chuck whipped his head down for a quick dive into the bowl. Luckily, the instructor told me not to hesitate the next time. You should keep walking. Whew...passed that one.

Another test, that my neighbor's dog failed, was that the owner must be out of the dog's sight for 1-3 minutes. They had to sit with strangers and be exposed to a lot of noise. John's dog got nervous, agitated and was whining. He failed.

Chuck fell asleep.

We passed.

On to our Certified Therapy Dog career.

LABS LOVE FOOD

First, I must note that Chuck's love of food knew no boundaries.

His food, your food, someone else's food, food on the floor, food in a garbage can, cat food in someone else's garage, the smell of food and so on.

Lab Fact

Labrador Retrievers are well known for their love affair with food, but scientists believe their overeating behavior might actually be a result of a genetic fault instead of just the generosity of their owners. *The New Daily*

Though not all food-obsessed dogs had the gene mutation, it was still a clear connection. And in a fascinating detail, the study also found that the gene mutation was more likely in Labradors that were working as assistance dogs. "It was surprising," University of Cambridge researcher Eleanor Raffan said in a statement "It's possible that these dogs are more food-motivated and therefore more likely to be selected for assistance-dog breeding programs, which historically train using food rewards." The gene mutation was only present in Labrador retrievers and flat coat retrievers. *Good Housekeeping.com*

CHUCK MEETS HIS DOUBLE

A Pudgy Pig

One day,
Chuck met a real pig!

I did not want to point out that they looked very much alike.

He saw it across the field and started running towards the little guy! Chuck froze and just stared at the pig since he did not move. The pudgy pig did not even look up, the owner said "It's ok, he doesn't care". So, they ended up walking around the park together for a while.

FIRST SOME PRACTICE

Thrown out of the Nursing Homes

To get some experience in an unthreatening place, I took Chuck to some Independent Living Homes. I was a little nervous and emotional because I wanted him to do well. I felt like I was taking my 5-year-old to kindergarten. Proud of his official Certified Therapy Dog title, proud of my accomplishment of training him and knowing that he would make a difference in someone's day. Our rounds included walking down the halls and outside patios greeting those that wanted love and attention.

Mr. Jones

We entered the first assisted living home. Everyone is smiling and so happy to see a big yellow lab prancing in with his wagging tail that could knock over an entire table of bricks.

The volunteer coordinators and techs escorted us, and their first idea was "Mr. Jones!". "Oh Mr. Jones will LOVE to meet Chuck…he needs a friend". He was in a wheelchair sitting by himself in a hall. His head was slumped over. Totally still but his eyes were open. I am holding Chuck on his long leash but talking to our hosts. Suddenly they are all smiling and letting out 'ewwwes' and 'awwwes' exclaiming that Chuck *Loves* Mr. Jones. The love was assumed because Chuck was licking Mr. Jones' hands, legs, arms…chewing on his sweater. Everyone is ecstatic! Somehow, I just knew there was a catch. I walked over to look, and Chuck was gleefully licking a ton of breadcrumbs off his body. Maybe Chuck really did love him – the food being a bonus. Bottom line – Mr. Jones was thrilled. The techs were beaming, and I was proud and relieved that we pulled off our first Certified Therapy Dog session.

Garbage Can & TV Stand Caper
Our next visit was to a local nursing home.

As I mentioned earlier, food was at the base of Chuck's reason to live. The techs told us which residents would like a visit in their rooms and the first one was a sweet lady that was sitting on the side of her bed smiling and waiting for the nice doggie to visit. Chuck excitedly walked in and made a b-line for her little garbage can. He pulled out all the food wrappers and her unfinished food. Trash everywhere. It happened so quickly that I did not have time to pull him back and gain that all important control. The nice lady thought it was funny. The techs did not. At least I do not think they did. I did not want to ask.

On to Room #2.
An old man in casual clothes with a sweet smile was sitting in his chair with his lunch on a TV stand. Chuck politely went over to greet the fellow, then tried to grab his lunch turkey sandwich off the table. There were many ***"I'm so sorry"*** remarks as we left….

A few sweet moments though!

Chuck jumped up on the arm of a chair and tried to kiss a 104-year-old beautiful lady. She threw her head back and laughed. At least I hope she was laughing and not trying to get away from his bad breath ☺

Personal Visits Included

We also visited other assisted living locations. A friend's father, Mr. Edge, enjoyed a quick game of tug-of-war with Chuck. Then they enjoyed happy hour ☺

Lessons learned.

The visits came to a halt, and we retired from the retirement homes.

Student Therapy: We even tried giving college students some comfort as they prepared for their final exams. We sat in the common court and the students stopped by to pet the dogs. Our visits were on the Wingate College campus in Monroe, North Carolina.

Chuck was overshadowed (literally) though by two huge Newfoundland dogs. Cuteness does matter in this business.

Several students expressed their joy at seeing the dogs and shared that it helped them reduce stress.

READY FOR THE BIG LEAGUE

The First Interview after Certification for Hospitals

We made a few more attempts to discover our best avenue for therapy dog work. We tried a Library – "Reading" with a child. The concept was that he would lay down and a child would read to him. The goal was that the dog would act interested and the child would feel comfortable. Chuck fell asleep.

The next big step was the hospitals. They recruited us to join the volunteer dogs at what is now Atrium Health Pineville Hospital. I had to sit through eight long hours of an orientation class while all Chuck had to do was go to an interview. They needed to check his temperament and his ability to mind me. He was able to respond to the volunteer coordinators' questions and commands until the very end.

Chuck was approved and asked to Shake-on-the-Deal. He blankly stared at her. I forgot to teach him that command, so I told her sorry, we don't know that one. We will work on it.

And we did. It became one of his five tricks.

TAILS OF LOVE FROM THE HOSPITAL

Now It Is A Job

Our first day. We entered with pride while also wondering where to start.

"We're supposed to do what now?"

In the orientation, I was instructed to walk the halls and could only enter rooms if we were asked.

Per the HIPPA laws, if I ran into someone I knew, I could speak to them but could not ask why they were there.

Not cool to yell out …

"Heyyyy…. the nose hair exams are down the hall ☺"

Always the Prankster

Our first assignment was to walk the halls on the 4th floor. One patient invited us in to say hello and we had a nice chat. After leaving the room, I noticed Chuck had big puffy cheeks…something was in his mouth. It was a pair of the guy's socks that he stole off the chair. I turned around and told the nurse I was so sorry and that I'd make him drop the contraband, but she laughed and said no, that's ok…. He can keep them, which made sense. Who wants a pair of slobbery socks?

Chuck carried them in his mouth for the rest of our visit.

A dog's tail can be a dangerous wrecking ball

As we continued our rounds, we walked through a lounge area where people were waiting for someone in surgery. There was a grouping of people in chairs and couches and one guy motioned me to bring Chuck over. Although I tried to keep a watch on his movements and anticipate what might happen, I did not react soon enough as he walked into the group wagging his tail so hard that it knocked the guy's arm as he was getting ready to drink his coffee. The guy was NOT happy.

Chuck the wrecking ball" continued swiftly because he heard a lady opening a bag of chips. The lady didn't see him coming. She looked up and screamed "…get him OUT of here!!!" She scared the whole waiting area and now people were looking at us in fear.

We turned around offering apologies as Chuck's tail swiped a newspaper out of another guy's hand.

Childhood Flashback

This swiftness of mischief reminded me of one of our childhood Labs, Deuce. One Thanksgiving my dad and brother Jeff filled their plates and went into the living room to watch some football. They put their plates down on the coffee table and went back to the kitchen for their southern iced tea. Upon return, their plates were empty. In that short period of time, Deuce had completely cleaned their plates…and any crumbs on the floor.

As an example; Chuck quickly ate the last of an appetizer.

Do not leave a Labrador unattended around food ☺

TOUCHING AND SAD MOMENT

The Power of a Dog's Presence

A Lovely Bed Visit:

One day we heard a faint voice calling us. Down the hall a lady stood in front of her door at the hospital and motioned us to come back. She had a beautiful face, was bald and battling cancer. Her one request was that Chuck get on the bed with her so she could hold and pet him. She missed her dogs and could not see them. We visited her several times after that and one day she asked for my contact information. She wanted Chuck to visit her at home when she was discharged. I gave her the information but never heard anything. I found out that she died several days later.

He did enjoy affection. I always wondered if he sensed her impending death. Chuck brought her comfort…. just by taking a break (nap).

MEDICAL DETECTION DOGS

It has been shown that dogs have uncanny abilities to detect medical issues, such as cancer, oncoming episodes of medical crisis (such as seizures), or anxiety. There is anecdotal evidence that dogs can also sense death, but how they process and perceive this information is still being debated and researched. *PetMD*

Dogs have a highly developed sense of smell, and some can detect the odor signatures of various types of cancer. Dogs have also shown they can detect colon cancer, prostate cancer, breast cancer, and melanoma by sniffing people's skin, bodily fluids, or breath.

Imperial College London

Into the ER – STAT!

ER Assignment

Months later, the hospital volunteer director asked me if Chuck would be 'ok' going into the ER area. I had to assume Chuck would not have an opinion about it. Off we went to the ER.

I honestly think it was more for the staff's mental health. The patients had more to worry about, and the visitors very rarely asked us to come into their rooms.

One day two very large police officers came walking by and they stopped in mid stride. I asked if I could take a picture of them with my big guy. They played along and agreed to escort him out of the ER ☺.

Kind of like a Perp Walk

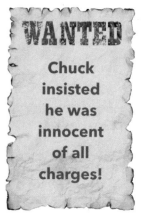

WANTED

Chuck insisted he was innocent of all charges!

A SPECIAL RECRUITMENT THAT CHANGED LIVES

After a year-and-a-half of hospital work, the volunteer director asked us to come to her office. Uh-Oh I thought. I hope we haven't done anything wrong… or gotten caught for it ☺.

It was a very special request. The question was directed to Chuck, which was interesting.

The question was posed to me in this way:

"Would Chuck mind going to our Mental Health Hospital on Billingsley Drive? They do not have therapy dogs visiting as no one wants to bring their dog there." I paused before answering because I wasn't sure **how** to **'ask'** Chuck if he would like to visit another hospital. I mean… dogs are smart, but can they express an opinion? ☺

I took the initiative to say "sure, we'll give it a try"!

It ended up being an eight-year love affair with many funny, warm and miraculous stories to share.

INITIAL PHONE CALL FROM THE MENTAL HEALTH HOSPITAL

I received a phone call from Tracey, the Director of Special Services. He wanted to talk to me about the hospital and what we would encounter. Tracey explained that they have different wings for the patients – young 5-12, teenagers 13-17, older adults in different wings – and that I needed to understand that the patients may be "schizophrenic, psychotic, depressed, multiple personalities etc."

Without thinking I replied, "No problem – they're like most of my friends".

I froze. 'Oh gosh', I thought, 'he's going to think I'm horrible'. I feebly said, "I'm sorry". He laughed and said,

> "Not to worry if you don't have a sense of humor, it would be hard to do this job".

During the 1960s, the first formal research involving animal therapy began.

Dr. Boris Levinson found that his dog had a positive effect on mentally impaired young patients. Specifically, he discovered that these patients were more comfortable and likely to socialize with his dog than with other humans.

Therapy dogs are sometimes called 'comfort dogs.' They support a person's mental health by providing attention and comfort. Their sweet demeanors and unconditional love may have a therapeutic benefit to those who face difficult health challenges. Unlike service dogs, however, anyone can enjoy a therapy dog.

JUST STARE INTO MY EYES...

Dogs have proven to be helpful in treating people with anxiety. This is one of the key reasons therapy dogs are among the most common therapy animals. **Studies have shown that looking into the dog's eyes boosts the production of dopamine and other neurochemicals in our body.**

Just stare into my eyes...your neurochemicals will thank you.

CHUCK'S FIRST DAY ON THE JOB

And Our First Miracle

After my first day of orientation, Chuck started his extraordinary job as the greatest therapy dog in the world. There were three of us and our first stop was the children's wing and as soon as we went through the doors

a little girl, maybe nine years old was walking the hall with a tech. She was catatonic. No life in her eyes or movement. We stopped for a moment and our tech was explaining the layout. During that time, Chuck was standing still and the little girl came up to him, started petting him on the head and looking at his volunteer badge. I was paying attention to the staff.

The tech and little girl whispered to each other and then we walked on.

When we left the wing and the door closed.

The Director looked at me and said, "That was the FIRST time that the little girl has spoken since being here".

She was asking if she could take his badge to her room and put it on her wall.

Tracey said it was also the most interactive she had been since being there. I call that our first miracle.

Sadly, we saw her several more times through the years as she had suffered much trauma. Chuck always recognized her! The experience I quickly learned was that Chuck (basic therapy dogs) don't really have to do anything. They are just *there* and provide some incredible undefined comfort to people. In Chuck's case, his goofy presence.

FROM HERE: SHORT ANECDOTES

So Many. We Will Choose the Best

First: Chuck's "Crew"

Throughout our eight years of visiting, we worked with the same techs. Sarah and Antroine were his main pack. They escorted him through the adult wings, so they became very close.

Goldie Loved Chuck!

Chuck mistakenly thought it was *Bring your Alligator to Work* day with Sarah and Antroine.

First Stop - Checking In

Chuck sincerely loved his job. I never made him do anything that he didn't want to do. He hated big chairs, boxes going over his head or loud noises. As soon as I said, "Let's go see the kids at the hospital", he jumped in the back seat of our Chuck Mobile SUV and off we went.

Or sometimes he rode shotgun!

He had to go through security, check in and then he went on to show off his 5-best-and only-tricks for the patients and staff.

Chuck loved it so much and especially got excited going to Atrium Behavioral Health because he got to see Antroine, Sarah, Maggie and the kids.

One day he was so wound up that he was dancing, jumping and whining in the lobby. Everyone noticed. Antroine said, "Is Chuck ok?" He got so out of control that the leash slipped out of my hand. He ran over to two police officers that were talking to a patient. He lunged for one of their gun holsters. "Yippee he thought...tug of war!" I was mortified.

I finally took him outside before we started our rounds so, he could run off some energy. I unhooked his leash to let him run down the sidewalk while saying OUTLOUD "What is *wrong* with you...are you crazy? You are acting like a nut bag!"

Yes, I really said that out loud...

Of course, there was a lady walking behind me, and I am sure she was thinking 'Who's the silly one here lady?'

Chuck's Five Tricks

As previously mentioned, family therapy dogs really do not have to do anything fun or special. They just need to love being loved. However, we felt it important that Chuck contributes more than just his handsome self.

Play Dead!

Not a really good one to use at nursing homes.

Go Find!

His human girlfriend, Chris D., taught him this game. Chris had Golden Retrievers, so she knew how to motivate them. A 'captive' audience favorite. I wanted to illustrate how strong a dog's sense of smell can be. He would stay

outside the room where the patients are waiting. I would go in and hide treats around the room. Just think how many smells would be in the snack room. Then we brought him in and I commanded **Go Find!** His record was 17 seconds.

Labrador Retrievers can smell 10,000 times better than you. While all dogs rely heavily on their sense of smell, Labs have especially strong schnozzes. These dogs can sniff out avalanche victims buried several feet beneath the snow, and they can detect odors that even some of our most advanced technology can't. They even have a high success rate of detecting cancer.

Control

I held up the treat in one hand and put out my other hand, palm out (like stop), with the command "CONTROL". Chuck would only watch the hand with the palm facing him. He would wait for me to snap my fingers. In the meantime, I would place some treats in strategic areas. A SNAP of the fingers and although he never looked to see *where* I put them he immediately found them. Another crowd favorite.

SPEAK!

If given the command to SPEAK!, Chuck would bark and he had a REALLY loud bark. 'His buddy, Antroine,' at the Mental Health hospital loved for me to give that command without telling the patients what would happen. Antroine LOVED the reactions. People screeched, bolted out of the room and one lady jumped up on a chair. Not unethical I guess….. ☺ I actually taught him how to bark out how old he was. We only made it to 6 though.

Costume Dress-Up

Chuck liked to be festive and did not mind most of his outfits. Dr. Seuss was a hit, but the Lion Head was the best! People would almost scream because it looked so realistic.

Dogs were highly valued in ancient Rome, as they were in other cultures, and the Roman dog served many of the same purposes as it did in, say, Egypt and Persia - as hunters, guardians, and companions - but with a **significant difference in focus.**

The ancient Egyptians and others of the Near East believed that dogs were **spiritual beings, similar to humans**, and they were "often associated with particular deities and the powers they wield".

Teenagers

Chuck's visit to the mental health hospital resulted in a breakthrough with two of the Autistic teenagers.

One of them would not let Chuck near him until Chuck won him over. He's always had a problem with "NO!" The young man pet Chuck slowly. Feeling a rhythm that only they could feel.

Maybe given courage, the other fella walked the lumbering polar bear down the hall. Interestingly, both wanted to stay close to the wall. That will become something I observed with Chuck through the years. He needed to walk close to the wall.

The staff was thrilled.

So was I.

How Does Chuck Make You Feel?

"Dogs have a magic effect on you, you can feel their love and that just makes you feel better inside you." **Mentally Ill Prisoner**

During one visit to the teenager's meeting room a young lady asked me, "How do therapy dogs make you feel"?

I thought about it and replied, "Well how does he make *YOU* feel"?

She broke out with a beautiful smile and said, "He makes me feel HAPPY"!

I smiled back with the quip "Well, there you go".

Sadly, I later noticed that she had cut marks all over her arms and slashes on her wrists. Those are moments that I cherish because I realized that Chuck truly did bring moments of pure joy.

Pet Therapy and Teenagers

Animal-assisted therapy is common in many children's hospitals as it is known to encourage adolescents to improve interactions with family and staff, take their medication more easily, calm nerves during or prior to painful or frightening procedures, etc. Pet therapy for teenagers facilitates a human-animal bond that delivers an array of scientifically documented benefits, some of which include: Boosts mood, Improves immune system, Enhances self-esteem, Builds positive social skills. *Pacific Teen Treatment*

The Hanging Incident

They say eyewitness accounts are unreliable. Our perceptions of what *really* happened may be skewed. As it relates to this incident, that was a good thing…. for me.

One afternoon we were visiting the men's side of the adult wing and a very tall soft-spoken guy with very intense, but kind eyes approached us. He kindly asked if he could walk Chuck. I said "yes" because I allowed that as it is a real treat for patients of all ages. The guy slowly turned down the hall and then took a sharp right towards his room. He said he wanted to take Chuck with him. Alarms went off inside me. I firmly but nicely said "NO". The Tech said "NO".

Then the guy started pulling the leash straight up and Chuck's neck was being pulled like a noose. His front legs are now lifted off the floor. He weighed about 120 lbs. Techs were called and commotion ensued as they tried to subdue him.

I reached into the middle of the mayhem and simply unhooked the leash from his collar and we walked quickly down the hall and out the door.

I paid close attention to Chuck's demeanor. Ears back? Hair on his back up? Looking me in the eyes for reassurance? Whimpering? NOPE.... he was prancing down the hall undisturbed, thought it was great fun!

That night I got a call from the hospital apologizing and asked if CHUCK was ok? Note: Chuck, not me. ☺I said "Oh, Chuck thought it was just someone having fun with him. I didn't think that the fellow wanted to actually hang him or hurt him, he just wanted his new friend to himself".

The Director quietly replied, "I'm glad you see it that way". As in, my eyewitness account may not be accurate? ☺

The whole hospital had been alerted. The next time we visited, everyone asked how he was and said they were so sorry.

In Chuck's words:

> **'Walk softly but carry a big stick'**

We experienced so much during our years of visiting hospitals. People who never spoke or smiled did so when Chuck walked in. People who never even came out of their room would come out for his visits. The children loved to pet him, make him speak and would draw an outline of their hands next to Chuck's huge paw. The big highlight was the chance to walk him down the hall by themselves. The teenagers who acted bored at first would start interacting and smiling. The kids loved to chase him around the yard. He even had birthday parties and cards.

BRANCHING OUT

Mixing Up Our Visiting Venues

Our love was the Atrium Behavioral Center and working with the mentally ill, however, Chuck needed to be experienced in other circumstances. After some discussion, which can be done with a dog if you know how to communicate. Not that they actually know what you are saying!

I call it the Fortune Cookie Method. After ordering Chinese food, we would put the three cookies on the floor. He could choose which one he wanted. His usual method was; smell all three, go to the one he preferred and nose it away from the others.

I used the idea of letting him choose by observing Chuck's demeanor as we visited other hospitals and facilities. We would go once or twice, and I could tell by his excitement or lack of interest by his demeanor.

As an example, he did not mind the retirement homes, but there wasn't much for him to do at the facilities we visited. Chuck loved the people at the Cancer Institute, however he had a fear of the halls. He loved the Children's Home. He loved Antroine, Sarah, Maggie, Christine and the people and patients at Atrium Behavioral Health.

Chuck the Rock Star –
Visiting a Children's Home

When I was attending high school my mom and I would sometimes pass a Children's Home in Charlotte. It was a large cold brick multi-floor orphanage. It was eerie and bothered me. My mother made a comment one day and said, "This home really bothers you, doesn't it?" It had a church in the front, and it was set back off the road. No movement. 'Sad', I thought. That was in the '70s.

As Chuck and I searched for new ways to spread his aura of love, I thought of visiting a Children's Home. We visited Alexander Children's Home in Charlotte, and it is a WONDERFUL place.

Chuck loved kids, action and the possibility of treats. Perfect Combo ☺

We got invited to one of the campuses, which has a big yard in the middle, one story buildings with individual rooms for the kids, a gym, craft areas and a picnic area. Some of the children were orphans but most were there for help, protection, or behavior issues and sadly sometimes no-one wanted them.

On our very first trip a boy about 11 came up with a huge smile and excitedly said "I remember CHUCK!... Do you remember me? Does he remember me?" I didn't at first but then remembered he had also been at the Mental Health Hospital. No-one wanted him. Unfortunately, I was to see this young boy over-and-over again.

The kids went crazy when I brought Chuck out. In a frenzy, they yelled Chuck! Chuck! Chuck! Chuck! Forget about me!

Their favorite thing to do was tell him to SPEAK and then he got a lot of treats!!! He would wait patiently for the command.

"It will be ok little buddy. Just talk to me all you want."

One of the most touching moments that I experienced. Chuck patiently walked with the young boy all around the field.

LEVINE'S CANCER INSTITUTE

Getting Hugs, Giving Hugs & Hugging the Wall

**Am I in your way?
By the way...
Whatcha eating?**

At Levine's Cancer Institute in Charlotte, we were asked to visit the second floor, which is where people get their chemo treatments.

And once again, Chuck did not mind asking for food, regardless of the patient's treatment.

My friends John, and Ingrid, invited us for a visit.

This is another plus for therapy dog work with your dog.

You can help friends.

Rock star greetings and even recognition.

This area is a big room with small seating areas for patients and family members. We passed by one couple.

They called out "Chuck!!!...we know you"!

I did not have any recognition of them and felt kind of bad. It turned out they were friends of our neighbor and knew us from walking and visiting with those neighbors when they were also there.

A couple of weeks later I was walking a dog and Chuck in another neighborhood. Some people were sitting in their driveway having a few beers. I waved and we chatted for a minute.

One of them said "Oh yes…we know Chuck". Again, I'm thinking *'how'*? They also knew that same neighbor.

We walked on and another couple invited us for a visit. He spent his time going cubicle to cubicle waiting for handouts. Seems like a "enough about you, what about me" attitude.

One last amusing moment ....

They also had little rooms separated by a curtain. People were in chairs or on beds receiving more severe treatments. I was talking to a nurse, so my back was to Chuck. He suddenly used his powerful head and nose to push open the curtain to check it out. A poor guy was half-naked, exposed and totally startled. But you know what? He started laughing. Our job was done.

We could also say hello to people waiting on the ground floor.

Sometimes Chuck would exhibit strange behavior. Even strange for him. For some reason he *had* to walk down the halls hugging the wall. Total body against it. He was terrified of the hall areas. Vibrations, smells, openness? We'll never know.

Therapy Dog Sessions.
We could have made some money on the side ☺

Checking the Halls
Ending the Shift in His Dr. Seus Cat-in-the-Hat Uniform

EVERYONE NEEDS A FRIEND

Dogs can empathize with other dogs.

Chuck also had a unique calming presence with other animals. If your dog is a Therapy Dog, they can provide even more unique comfort.

Cats not so much (he was afraid of them), but he gave comfort to many other dogs and even small children!

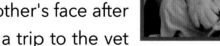

Dogs have their own cues for reading emotions in each other. Many of them are physical. But they will also seek each other out during times of stress or emotion. So, if you notice one dog licking the other's face after a trip to the vet or rubbing his body against the other during a thunderstorm, recognize it as their way of showing empathy. *Pet MD*

Lola at four months: A client asked if we could please watch her for the night. Scared to death. Chuck gently took good care of her.

CC - Chuck's little friend till the end

Sport - A friend to a fellow who had friend issues. He barely tolerated other dogs.

Amber

Very First Girlfriend

Bugsy - Chuck would walk her around the neighborhood.

Tasha - She was not crazy about other dogs but found his calmness therapeutic. She loved him even when he was gone and in heaven.

Nothing Better Than a Chuck Hug

Meiko   **Chino**   **Stevie**

**Kids just gravitated towards Chuck.
That's another good sign for a Therapy Dog.**

**Tuck – His one feline
'semi-friend' !**

TV STAR

Chuck's Presence Was Even Captured on the TV Screen

My company created a Charlotte market wide television campaign titled **'Bring Me Home Carolinas'.**

We helped over 1,000 animals get adopted out of the local shelters.

Chuck was the 'SpokesDog'.

Posing For The Camera

Very Patient – Waiting For His Call to the Set

Official Media Sponsor
wbtv.com/bringmehome

#WBTVandME

Humane Society
OF UNION COUNTY

www.hs-uc.org

Petsmart 6420 Weddington Rd, Wesley Chapel

**Join us as we open our doors
for a Spectacular Pet Adoption Event**

Saturday, April 8, 2017

10am till 2pm

(adoptions include 1 year Heart worm preventative)

Help us as we find homes for all of our animals!

ADOPTING PETS IN OUR COMMUNITIES

Bring Me Home Carolinas is the property of Vision Communications, Inc. This logo and title cannot be used or duplicated by other parties.

TIME TO RETIRE

Chuck was twelve-and-a-half so it was time to retire so he could enjoy himself.

Spend some time in Florida with his dad and Uncle Jimmy

Hang out by the pool or Jump in a Koi Pond

Go to the beach. Meet some cute girls who did not even know that he was sitting behind them ☺

Most importantly, Chuck will finally have some time to check-out the grocery specials! Food is everything.

CHUCK ENJOYED
HIS LIFE TO THE END

Now For the Hard Part

"Pets teach us the purest kind of love." –Unknown.

Saying Goodbye

REMEMBERING THE LOVE

You will experience incredible love every time you take your own therapy dog for a visit.

There are so many stories and pictures that represent the journey of *Chuck, The World's Greatest Therapy Dog*. It is hard to segue to what all pet owners have experienced.

November the 16th 2020 a Rainbow appears at our house. Chuck started acting funny and was very wobbly walking around our front yard. I took him inside, he laid down and stared at a wall, unresponsive to my voice. I finally asked him if he was hungry. At 120 lbs. that was always a, "Yes", answer. He got up slowly but would not eat. That is one sign that dogs are ready to go to heaven.

Bob took him to the emergency clinic, and they opened him up. Chuck had cancer and we did not want him to suffer. There was nothing they could do.

Your presence we miss
Your memory we treasure
Loving you always
In our thoughts forever...

For our all dear departed pets
who have crossed
The Rainbow Bridge

We said our goodbyes and thanked him for his love, goofy personality, service to us and to the world.

Chuck crossed over the Rainbow Bridge to wait for us.

WHY CHUCK HAS THE TITLE,

'The World's Greatest Therapy Dog'

I informed our friends at the Atrium Behavioral Health Hospital and a few days later, I got an email asking me to come by one afternoon. I thought they wanted to give me a big card or something, but it was that beautiful plaque. The staff assembled outside the building, and it was so moving.

My neighbors even collected money for the hospital in Chuck's name. It went towards a new gym.

Healthcare Professional Testimonies

All Dogs Breeds Are Welcome

"We love to have therapy dogs come to visit us because they bring so much joy. We were introduced to Chuck and Barbara many years ago and Chuck became one of the best and most anticipated therapy tools we could ever hope for. Therapy dogs provide calmness and unconditional affection. They are very helpful to the patients and staff! We had pictures of Chuck hanging in the dayroom for the kids to see, they would ask who he was and anticipate meeting him!"

Sarah, LRT,CTRS
Clinical Programming Manager
Inpatient Therapy Department

"Chuck, one of our very favorite therapy dogs, and I became fast friends. We work with people that are often sad and lonely, so therapy dogs. provide a very unique experience for our patients. My favorite trick was watching Barbara tell him to *speak!* It was so loud and funny that it made me smile also. We were very thankful for his visits."

Antroine

Activity Therapist

A FEW MORE THERAPY DOG STORIES!

Whopper

Yvonne: ***Whopper*** and I have been volunteering for 5 years. Whopper is a 135 lb Great Dane/Mastiff mix. We volunteer at elementary and high schools through PetPalsNC.com and colleges, military events, special needs camps, and some nursing homes.

During that time, we discovered everyone wanted to meet him and he loved people. You can't train a dog to love people. He would often lean against strangers while

they rubbed his ears. Sometimes, he even sits on their feet. It is a trait of his breed. We were told by one of his trainers that he would make a great therapy dog. And he WAS a great therapy dog!

Whopper is not allowed to go into hospitals because he does slobber some. We mostly visit elementary schools

and high schools. We also go to colleges, nursing homes, women's shelters, Night to Shine dances, and military events welcoming troops home or sending them off. In elementary schools, he works with kids for a variety of reasons, to reduce stress, listen to them read, or help them work through a problem.

At a nursing home, a lady came over and asked me to take him to her husband. He was suffering from some form of dementia. The wife put her husband's hand on Whopper's head. Slowly, he started petting Whopper. After a few minutes, he looked up and smiled. His wife was crying, his daughter was crying.

Charley

Johanna: **Charley** is an almost sixteen-year-old eighty-pound Golden Doodle. He has been a certified therapy dog since he was two years-old and he has brought countless amounts of joy to so many people. Charley's

owner, Johanna, is a former special education teacher. The best way Johanna found to motivate her students was to promise that Charley would visit the school to reward good behavior and effort.

After seeing how well Charley interacted with the children, Johanna decided to certify Charley as a therapy dog through Therapy Dog International. As a therapy dog, Charley has worked in nursing homes, in a group home for children, and he has done post-crisis grief support.

Charley's owner is now a clinical social worker, and Charley is a staple at her private practice.

Charley always greets people with a tail wag and a smile in his eyes! Charley is a loyal and loving dog that has an intuitive sense of when a person is hurting and how to help.

Animals can be incredibly healing for people with disabilities and individuals who have experienced trauma. A dog brings a special non-judgmental presence to every interaction.

Rosie

Johanna: **Rosie** is an eleven-month-old Golden Doodle with a very sweet disposition. The plan is

for Rosie to take her therapy dog test shortly after she turns one year old. Rosie has shown an incredible interest in children and is very in tune with their emotions. Johanna hopes to have Rosie work therapeutically with children that have disabilities.

She has three human siblings at home that Rosie showers with love on a daily basis. Johanna hopes to have Rosie work therapeutically with children that have disabilities.

A dog brings a special non-judgmental presence to every interaction. After seeing all the joy that Charley has brought to so many people, Johanna knew she wanted to train another dog to be a therapy dog.

Duncan

Shirley: **Duncan** is a fun and calm yellow Labrador Retriever that brings pleasure everywhere he goes. Because he loves attention and has a gentle personality, I decided to try therapy dog work with him. First, we took basic obedience classes to polish the commands he already knew. After earning his AKC Canine Good Citizen, we pursued therapy dog registration with Pet Partners.

Our very first visit took place at my church. The student pastor wanted a therapy dog team at the Longest Night Service (for those experiencing grief at the holidays). The senior pastor wasn't sure about having a dog in church, but approved the visit. After the service the pastor observed Duncan lean against the legs of a woman in tears while looking up into her eyes. He asked, "How does he know to do that?" I answered that Duncan's ability to read human emotion is what makes him an excellent therapy dog.

As a retired elementary teacher/media specialist, I focus most of our visits on the elementary students who need practice reading. At one school I was asked to work with a student who had some behavior problems. I agreed as long as his time with Duncan was never taken away as punishment. Even though I sometimes had to pick up the student from the principal's office, he spent some good days reading to Duncan while stroking his fur. I know that at times, reading with Duncan was the high point of his week.

Working with Duncan is as important to me as it is to everyone else! I have experienced great joy and a sense of purpose with this volunteer work. It has been a benefit to my health as well.

SOMETHING TO CHEW ON

During our 10 years of therapy dog work people would often remark that their dog would (or would not) be a good therapy dog. They also asked how I trained Chuck, or did they need to hire a trainer? I am not a professional trainer, so I am going to share some of the information provided by the wonderful Therapy Dog Certification sites. Once trained and certified, your only commitment is your time as the handler and as the limo driver ☺.

Therapy dogs are in such demand that you can work as much or as little as you like.

CERTIFICATION INFORMATION

Steps & Training for Certification Ideas

There are many Therapy Dog certification and training organizations to consider. Offered below are the requirements outlined by **Therapy Dogs International**. I was able to train Chuck myself, so I have provided a few tips that I used to get him ready for the test. However, people also hire a trainer to help them.

THE DOG MUST COMPLETE THESE 13 STEPS OF THE TDI TEST. DEMONSTRATING CONFIDENCE AND CONTROL

Note: At check-in, before beginning Test 1, the owner must present a current rabies certificate and any other state or locally required inoculation certificates and licenses. Prior to being admitted to the evaluation, a brief temperament test will be performed on the dog by the evaluator. Phase I The dog must wear either a flat buckle or snap-in collar (non-corrective) or a harness (non-corrective), all testing must be on a 6ft leash.*

TEST 1: TDI ENTRY TABLE (Simulated as a Hospital Reception Desk)

The dog/handler teams are lined up to be checked in (simulating a visit). The evaluator (volunteer coordinator) will go down the line of registrants and greet each new arrival including each dog. At the same time the collars will be checked, as well as other points.

TEST 2: CHECK-IN AND OUT OF SIGHT (Time: One Minute)

You will already know this about your dog.

An easy one to practice at someone's home.

The handler will start completing the paperwork. Once all teams have been placed, the helper(s) will ask the handler(s) if they can hold their dogs. Now the handler(s) will leave for "one minute". The handler(s) can give the "stay" command verbally or by hand signal or both. The helper(s) can talk to and pet the dog(s). The dog(s) can sit, lie down, stand or walk around within the confines of the leash.

TEST 3: GETTING AROUND PEOPLE

As the dog/handler team walks toward the 'patients' rooms, there will be various people standing around. Some of the people will try visiting with the dog. The dog/handler team must demonstrate that the dog can withstand the approach and touching by several people from all sides at the same time and is willing to visit and walk around a group of people.

We practiced this when I took a walk with a friend. Just ask your dog to Sit and then Stay. Drop the leash and walk about 6ft. Then turn around and have your friend give the command to go to you.

This one is very similar to 4 and 5. A longer line. You will ask your dog to stay.

We practiced this in our yard.

If your dog has neighborhood friends, you can ask the owner and dog to join you for fun and treats.

TEST 4: GROUP SIT/STAY

The evaluator will ask all the participants to line up with their dogs in a heel position. Now, the handlers will put their dogs in a sit/stay position. The handlers will give the sit command to the dogs. The evaluator will tell the handlers to leave their dogs. The handlers will step out to the end of their 6 ft. leash, turn around

and face the dog(s) and wait for the evaluator's command to return to their dog(s). (The evaluator will give the return command immediately).

TEST 5: GROUP DOWN/STAY Same as test number 4, except dogs will now be in a down/stay.

TEST 6: RECALL ON A 20 FT. LEASH

All handlers will be seated. Three dogs at a time will be fitted with a long line. The reason we fit more than one dog with a long line at the same time is to save time. The handler will continue to hold the 6 ft leash while the long line is fitted by a helper. One handler at a time will take the dog to a designated area which is out of reach of the other dogs even with a 20 ft. line. The evaluator will then give the command: Down your dog! The handler can down the dog either by voice and or by hand signal. The evaluator will give the command: Leave your dog! The handler will tell the dog to stay either by voice and/or by hand signal. The handler now will turn away from the dog and walk in a straight line to the end of the 20 ft. lead. The handler will turn and face the dog. The evaluator immediately will tell the handler to call the dog. The handler will call the dog, either by voice, hand signal or both.

TEST 7: VISITING WITH A PATIENT The dog should show willingness to visit a person and demonstrate that it can be made readily accessible for petting (i.e. small dogs will be placed on a person's lap or held; medium dogs will sit on a chair or stand close to the patient to be easily reached, and larger dogs will be standing).

TEST 8: TESTING OF REACTIONS TO UNUSUAL SITUATIONS The dog handler team will be walking in a straight line. The dog can be on either side, or

> When we were tested, they had maybe 7 people walking towards us. On crutches, in a wheelchair, talking loudly or rattling a walker.
>
> They were testing Chuck's calmness around distractions.
>
> At home I would drop some items when he wasn't looking. It is ok to be startled, they just can't start barking or run away.

If you know someone in an assisted living facility, you could visit and practice this one.

slightly behind the handler; the leash must not be tight. The evaluator will ask the handler to have the dog sit (the handler may say sit or use a hand signal or both).

Next the evaluator will ask the handler to down the dog (the handler may say down or use a hand signal or both). Next continuing walking in a straight line, the handler will be asked to make a right, left and an about turn at the evaluator's discretion. The following distractions will be added to the heel on a loose leash.

- The team will be passing a person on crutches.
- Someone running by calling "excuse me, excuse me" waving hands (this person is running up from behind the dog. It could also be a person on a bicycle, roller blades, or a skateboard etc).

Another person will be walking by and drop something.

- making a loud startling noise (a tin can filled with pebbles or a clipboard). At an indoor test there may be a running vacuum cleaner (realistic in a facility).

- Next the team will be requested to make an about-turn.

- And then a left turn.

- Then the team will be requested to make a right turn,

TEST 9: LEAVE-IT; PART ONE The dog handler/ team meets a person in a wheelchair. The dog should approach the person and visit. The person in the wheelchair, after briefly interacting with the dog, will offer the dog a treat by holding the treat steady in the hand while enticing the dog. The handler must instruct the dog to leave it. It is up to the handler as to what kind of verbal command they use to keep the dog from licking or taking the food. The handler should explain to the patient why the dog cannot eat a treat while visiting (i.e. dog has food allergies).

I did not think Chuck would be able to pass this one.

A bowl of food was on the floor, I walked over it and hesitated, which gave him the opening to grab some food. They told me not to hesitate.

Easy to practice at home.

TEST 10: LEAVE-IT; PART TWO The dog handler will be walking in a straight line with the dog at heel. There will be a piece of food in the path of the dog. The dog is not allowed to lick or eat the food. There should also be a bowl of water in the path of the dog. The dog is not allowed to drink.

TEST 11: MEETING ANOTHER DOG

A volunteer with a demo dog will walk past the dog handler/team, turn around and ask the handler a question. After a brief conversation, the two-handlers part.

TEST 12: ENTERING THROUGH A DOOR TO VISIT AT THE FACILITY

A person should be able to go through the entrance ahead of the dog/handler team. The dog handler team is ready to enter through a door to a facility. The handler first has to put the dog in a sit, stand, or down stay, whatever is most comfortable for the dog.

In 10 years, I generally did not see other dogs because of where we visited. It is important that your dog stays calm around other dogs.

Easy to practice at home or visiting a dog friendly establishment.

Ask neighbor-hood children to help by playing this game.

You could also see how your dog will do reading to a child or letting them hug.

TEST 13: REACTION TO CHILDREN The children will be running and yelling, playing ball, dropping objects, and doing what children usually do while playing.

1. The handler will walk with the dog past playing children (distance from the children must be at least 20 feet).

2. a. The dog must lie down beside the handler.

    b. The handler will simulate reading a book while the dog is lying down.

    c. The dog MUST have his back to the children.

EPILOGUE

I hope you enjoyed our stories and had a few laughs!
Maybe you also were touched by the special moments.

Most of all, I hope you will consider
helping *your* family dog become a Certified Therapy Dog.

If they have the temperament and you have the time,
It is an awesome gift to so many.

Written by:

Barbara D. Wilson
2024

Logo Design:

Jun Deen

Editing:

Beverly Deen

The End
and
A Kiss Goodbye